T0290167

ROMANIA DURING WORLD WAR I

OBSERVATIONS OF AN AMERICAN JOURNALIST

JOHN REED

ROMANIA DURING WORLD WAR I

OBSERVATIONS OF AN AMERICAN JOURNALIST

Edited, with an Introduction by A.K. Brackob

CENTER FOR
Romanian
STUDIES

Center for Romanian Studies
Las Vegas ◊ Chicago ◊ Palm Beach

Published in the United States of America by
Histria Books
7181 N. Hualapai Way, Ste. 130-86
Las Vegas, NV 89166 USA
HistriaBooks.com

The Center for Romanian Studies is an independent academic and cultural institute with the mission to promote knowledge of the history, literature, and culture of Romania in the world. The publishing program of the Center is affiliated with Histria Books. Contributions from scholars from around the world are welcome. To support the work of the Center for Romanian Studies, contact us at: info@centerforromanianstudies.com

All rights reserved. No part of this book may be reprinted or reproduced or utilized in any form or by any electronic, mechanical, or other means, now known or hereafter invented, including photocopying and recording, or in any information storage or retrieval system, without the permission in writing from the Publisher.

Library of Congress Control Number: 2018935325

ISBN 978-1-59211-002-5 (softbound)
ISBN 978-1-59211-006-3 (hardback)
ISBN 978-1-59211-128-2 (eBook)

Copyright © 2022 by Histria Books
All Rights Reserved

Table of Contents

Table of Contents

Introduction
JOHN REED IN ROMANIA

In 1915, American journalist John Reed traveled to Eastern Europe to cover the World War for *Metropolitan Magazine*. He had already established a name for himself through his vivid first-hand descriptions of the revolution in Mexico, in which he recounted his daring exploits while riding along with the legendary Pancho Villa. But Jack Reed found this new war to be far less romantic affair. Strong censorship and the conditions of war on the eastern front in Europe did not permit him to engage in the same sort of adventures he had experienced in Mexico. This was anathema to someone imbued with heroic ideals and a rebel spirit. Reed expressed his frustration with the situation when writing to his friend and former professor Charles Copeland:

> *Dear Cope:*
>
> *Circumstances of mailing-convenience, neutrality and so forth, force me always to return*

to Romania and the "Paris of the Balkans," though I detest the country and the people.

Imagine a small Paris in every essential respect – cafes, kiosks, pissoirs, an Academy occupied with producing a dictionary, Futurist painters and poets who are pederasts...politicians who are known by the mistresses they keep, craven newspapers, bawdy weeklies....

Your true Romanian boasts that there are more cocottes in Bucharest in proportion to the population than in any other two cities of the world. No one does anything but screw, drink and gabble....

Officers in salmon-pink and baby-blue uniforms...sit at cafes sipping ices and eating tartlets all day long and drive up and down the Calea Victoriei in cabs, winking at throngs of women.... There is a dinky Hohenzollern king, a dinky throne and court, a dinky aristocracy of fake Byzantine Emperor's spawn. Everybody is crooked... It reeks with millionaires, grown rich by hogging the oil wells or by the absentee ownership of vast lands where the peasants sweat out their lives for a franc a day....

If I ever saw a place ripe for revolution, this country is ripe. The peasants are a very fine and poetic people, but they are cowed.

I hate old Europe more every day. America's the place.[1]

Reed's socialist convictions partly explain his disgust with the bourgeois Romanian society he encountered in Bucharest. Although seemingly an unlikely candidate to become a radical leader, the Harvard educated journalist emerged as one of the leading revolutionaries of his day. Born into an upper middle-class family in Portland, Oregon on October 20, 1887, John Reed attended private schools in New Jersey before entering Harvard University in 1906. It was at Harvard where Reed first met Copeland who he would write "stimulated me to find color and strength and beauty in books and in the world and to express it."[2]

His radicalism began after he graduated from Harvard and became a journalist in New York. There he became the companion of the wealthy socialite

---

[1]quoted in Robert A. Rosenstone, *Romantic Revolutionary: A Biography of John Reed,* (New York, 1975), pp. 215-216.

[2]quoted in Bertram D. Wolfe, *Strange Communists I Have Known,* (New York, 1967), p. 15.

Mabel Dodge who introduced him to the leader of the
I.W.W. (Industrial Workers of the World), William D.
Haywood. As a result of this meeting, Reed covered
the famous silk worker's strike in Patterson, New Jersey where he was arrested for siding with striking
workers. A year later, in November, 1913, he was sent
to cover the revolution in Mexico for *Metropolitan
Magazine*. His reports from Mexico, where he accompanied the rebel army of Pancho Villa, won him praise
in America, placing him among the leading journal-
ists of his generation. As Bertram Wolfe noted: "His
reports overflow with life and movement: simple, sav-
age men, capricious cruelty, warm comradeship,
splashes of color, bits of song, fragments of social and
political dreams, personal peril, gay humor, reckless
daring."[3] Reed's innate talent for description made
his readers feel the events he recounted. His articles,
published in a volume later that same year under the
title, *Insurgent Mexico*, cemented his reputation as a
war correspondent.

While his romanticism, daring, and talent as a
writer won him accolades, his experiences with the
peasant armies of Pancho Villa further strengthened

---

[3]Wolfe, *Strange Communists*, p. 24.

his growing socialist convictions. It must be remembered that for intellectuals of this generation, which had not yet experienced the atrocities that would be committed in its name, the ideals of socialism held a romantic attraction, perhaps as they do today for many who no longer have a historical sense of the tragedy of collectivism. In a world filled with poverty and injustice and overcome with a sense of stagnation, the dream of a socialist society attracted many followers – among them the American journalist John Reed. In many ways, he is a representative figure of his generation – a generation searching for its identity, famously referred to by Ernest Hemingway, quoting Gertrude Stein, as the "lost generation." His former classmate at Harvard, Walter Lippman, described him best when he wrote in *The New Republic* in 1914:

> *He is many men at once, and those who have tried to bank on some phase of him, to regard him as a writer, a correspondent, a poet, a revolutionist, or a lover, lose him. There is no line between the play of his fancy and his responsibility to fact; he is for the time the person he imagines himself to be.*

Reed's personal opposition to the war – which he saw as a struggle between capitalist interests – did not prevent him from traveling to Europe to cover the war on the Eastern front for *Metropolitan Magazine*. A romantic at heart, Reed yearned for adventure and the war, he thought, opened worlds of possibility just as it had in Mexico. It was during this journey that he first came to Romania. His observations on the situation of the country in 1915, a year before its entry into the war on the side of the allies, are those of a radical American journalist, disgusted by the bourgeois society he observed in Bucharest. It must be remembered that while Reed's experiences in Romania were mainly limited to the capital city and the surrounding area, he also travelled in the Hapsburg lands and some of his observations, coming from a man who displayed no particular sympathy for the Romanian people, are especially interesting. For example, when discussing the question of Transylvania, Reed writes:

> *In Transylvania, the birthplace of the race, and the Banat beyond, there are some three million Rumanians. But there, in spite of the desperate Hungarian campaign to Magyarize the people as the Russians did in Bessarabia, the racial*

feeling is strong and growing. The Transylvanians are rich and civilized; when the Rumanian tongue was banned in the higher schools and churches, they fought a stubborn fight, crossing the mountains into Rumania for education, and spreading the nationalist propaganda at home and abroad so thoroughly that every Rumanian knows and feels for his oppressed brothers on the other side of the Carpathians, and you can travel across Hungary as far as Buda-Pesth and beyond without speaking any language but Rumanian.

Reed's travels in Eastern Europe formed the basis for his volume *The War in Eastern Europe*, published by Charles Scribner's Sons in New York in 1916. The book contained a series of drawings by Boardman Robinson, who accompanied Reed on his journey, meant to evoke the atmosphere the two Americans encountered in each of the countries described in the book. Still he failed to recapture the romanticism he had encountered in Mexico amidst the staleness of trench warfare in Europe. As Bertram Wolfe pointed out, "His tour of duty as a European war correspondent was a disappointment to editors, friends, and to Jack himself."[4]

After returning to the United States, and dissatisfied with his travels in Eastern Europe, Reed again set out for Europe in August of 1917, this time inspired by the revolutionary changes taking place in Russia. It was here that he, together with his wife, Louise Bryant, bore witness to the Bolshevik revolution which he believed would give birth to the socialist utopia he envisioned. Reed was not merely an observer of the historic events in Russia, but also a participant in them. He whole-heartedly supported the Bolshevik cause, working in the Bureau of International Revolutionary Propaganda for a time after the establishment of the Soviet regime. Before his return home, Leon Trotsky appointed him as the first Russian consul to the United States, but the designation was subsequently withdrawn due to fierce opposition from the American Embassy.

He finally returned to the United States in April of 1918. While American customs officials initially

---

[4]Wolfe, Strange Communists, p. 25.

confiscated the materials he brought back from Russia, Reed eventually recovered them and proceeded to write his most famous book, *Ten Days that Shook the World*. It is this eyewitness account of the events that rocked Russia, which the British scholar Eric Homberger called, "perhaps the most remarkable account of a revolution ever to have been written by an eyewitness,"[5] that is John Reed's lasting claim to fame. It has been translated into numerous languages. The partisan nature of the book is clear; Reed never attempts to hide his sympathy for the Bolshevik cause. Despite this, he manages to evoke the historic events in Russia during the fall of 1917 in such a way so as to transcend his own sense of partisanship and bring to life those heady for generations of readers. Jack Reed fully utilizes the remarkable talent he had demonstrated in his reports from Mexico in his account of the Bolshevik revolution. The book won praise from Lenin and the Soviet leader even wrote a short preface to it.

Inspired by what he had experienced in Russia, Reed began to take a more active role in American politics, joining the Socialist Party of America. As with

---

[5]see Eric Homberger, "Messenger for Revolution," in *The Times Higher Education Supplement,* 17 March 1989, p.13.

other socialist movements in the world in the wake of
the Bolshevik revolution, the American left began to
split into factions once the war had ended. In 1919,
Reed was among those who broke away from the Socialist Party and founded Communist Labor Party of
America. At the same time, another socialist faction
formed a rival Communist Party. As each side in this
struggle between communist factions sought to gain
legitimacy by obtaining recognition from the Comintern, John Reed was sent as the delegate of the Communist Labor Party to obtain recognition for the party
in Moscow. He would never again set foot in the
United States.

Failing to obtain recognition for his party from the
Comintern, which ordered the two rival American
communist factions to unite, Reed attempted to return home in the spring of 1920 amidst the civil war
that raged in Russia at the time. He was arrested and
imprisoned in Finland. Lenin and the Soviets inter-
vened and secured his release and he returned to
Russia in June of 1920. Having temporarily abandoned plans to return to the United States, Reed
worked in the Comintern, being selected as a member
of the executive committee sent to the Congress of
Peoples of the East in Baku. During this trip, he con-
tracted typhus. He returned to Moscow in September

to find that his wife, Louise Bryant, herself a remarkable journalist, had made the hazardous journey to Russia to join him. Their reunion was short-lived; Reed soon fell ill and died in October, 1920. He was buried in the Kremlin wall, one of only three Americans to have been so honored by the Soviet regime.

Near the end of his life, as he saw the revolution begin to devour its own and stifle dissent, John Reed's enthusiasm for Bolshevism waned. His frequent clashes with Zinoviev in the Comintern drained the Harvard educated intellectual. Reed was a romantic revolutionary by nature, and as the Russian revolution morphed into a highly bureaucratic and oppressive regime that strived to snuff out the last vestiges of revolutionary ferver, he began to feel alienated by it. The English sculptress Claire Sheridan, who met him in Moscow shortly before he fell ill, wrote in her diary how out of place Reed seemed to her, "I understand the Russian spirit, but what strange force impels an apparently normal young man from the United States?"[6] Perhaps Betram Wolfe answered that query and summed it up best went he wrote: "John Reed's spirit evades official control and

---

[6]Ibid.

goes its own characteristic way. It lives on in the record of his rebellious, adventurous, generously romantic, perpetually immature, brave poet's life."[7] His writings on Romania form part of that record.

ᘔᘔᘔ

While John Reed is internationally known for his famous account of the Bolshevik Revolution, *Ten Days that Shook the World*, which has also appeared in a Romanian edition,[8] his writings about Romania are virtually unknown. As a journalist of great talent and an eyewitness to the situation in the country in 1915, on the eve of its entry into the war, his accounts are worth reading for those who are interested in this period of Romanian history or in the author himself. While his observations on the country are based largely on the time he spent in the capital city, Reed anticipated this criticism:

> "It will be said that I have judged Rumanians
> by the people of Bucarest, and that Bucarest is
> not all Rumania. But I insist that the metropolis

---

[7] Wolfe, *Strange Communists*, p. 35.

[8] see John Reed, *Zece zile care au zguduit lumea*, (București: ESPLP, 1957), 340 pp. 2nd edition, (București: Editura politică, 1962).

*reflects the dominant traits of any nation – that
Paris is essentially French, Berlin essentially
Prussian, and Bucarest thoroughly Ruma-
nian."*

John Reed's writings on Romania are comprised
of two principal texts. The first, "Rumania in Difficul-
ties," is a chapter from his book, *The War in Eastern
Europe*, originally published in 1916. The second,
"The Rights of Small Nations," is from a posthumous
volume of stories entitled, *Daughter of the Revolution
and Other Stories*, edited by Floyd Dell and published
in 1927. In addition to these, I have added an article
that John Reed published in an American newspa-
per, the *New York Mail*, in 1917 under the title, "Roumanian Soldier Finds His Way from Russian Front to
America."

Finally, although it contains no information
about John Reed and Romania, I have appended
Louise Bryant's account of the death of her husband
in Moscow because it is a little-known document of
great historical value for those interested in the life of
John Reed. The original spelling used by the author
in each of the texts presented here has been retained.

A.K. Brackob

ROMANIA
DURING
WORLD WAR I

JOHN REED

John Reed (1887-1920)

RUMANIA IN DIFFICULTIES*

My window, high up in the dazzling neo-French fa-
çade of the Athenée Palace Hotel in Bucarest, looks
down on a little park smothered in almost tropical
luxuriance of trees and flowers, where busts of minor
Rumanian celebrities on marble columns stonily ig-
nore each his marble wreath proffered by the lan-
guishing Muse kneeling on the pedestal. You've seen
millions like them all over France. To the left lies the
Atheneul, combining the functions of the Louvre, the
Pantheon, and the Trocadero, and built to suggest
the architecture of the Paris Opera. Its baroque dome
bears aloft a frieze of gilt lyres, and the names of the
great dead in gilt letters: Shakespeare, Cervantes,

*from John Reed, *The War in Eastern Europe*, pictured by
Boardman Robinson, (New York, 1916), pp. 295-308.

Pushkin, Camoens, Beethoven, Racine, etc., and two or three Rumanians unknown to the West. Eastward as far as one can see, red-tile roofs and white-stone copings pile up, broken with vivid masses of trees – palaces and mansions and hotels of the most florid modern French style, with an occasional Oriental dome or the bulb of a Rumanian Greek church. It is like a pleasure city built by Frenchmen in the south, this little "Paris of the Balkans," whose Rumanian name, Bucureshti, means literally "City of Joy."

At sunset the town wakes from the baking heat of a cloudless summer day. On the right the principal and smartest street, Calea Victoriei, winds roaring between the High-Life Hotel (pronounced "Hig-Liff") and the Jockey Club building – which might have been bodily transplanted from the Boulevard Haussman. All the world is driving home from the races down on the Chaussée – a combination of the Bois de Boulogne and the Champs Elysées – where it has seen the stable of Mr. Alexandre Marghiloman, chief of the Germanophile branch of the Conservative party, win the Derby as usual – one, two, three. The regular evening parade begins. An endless file of handsome carriages, drawn by superb pairs of horses, trots smartly by in both directions along the twisting, narrow street. The coachmen wear blue-velvet robes to their feet, belted with bright satin ribbons whose ends flutter out behind, so you can guide them right or left by pulling the proper tab. These are public cabs owned communally by their drivers, who are all members of a strange Russian religious sect expelled from their own country; their belief requires that after they have married and had one child, they shall become eunuchs....

Each carriage is the setting for a woman or two women, rouged, enamelled, and dressed more fantastically than the wildest poster girl imagined by French decorators. A dense crowd overflowing from the sidewalks into the street moves slowly from the Atheneul up past the King's palace to the boulevards and back again – extravagant women, and youths made up like French decadent poets, and army officers in uniforms of pastel shades, with much gold lace, tassels on their boots, and caps of baby-blue and salmon-pink-color combinations that would make a comic-opera manager sick with envy. They have puffy cheeks and rings under their eyes, these officers, and their cheeks are

sometimes painted, and they spend all their time riding up and down the Calea with their mistresses, or
eating cream puffs at Capsha's pastry-shop, where all
prominent and would-be prominent Bucarestians
show themselves every day, and where the vital affairs of the nation are settled. What a contrast between the officers and the rank and file of the army –
strong, stocky little peasants who swing by in squads
to the blare of bugles, excellently equipped and
trained! The numberless cafés and pastry-shops spill
tables out the sidewalk and the streets, crowded with
debauched-looking men and women got up like cho-
rus-girls. In the open café-gardens the gypsy orches-
tras swing into wild rhythms that get to be a habit
like strong drink; a hundred restaurants fill with ex-
otic crowds. Lights flash out. Shop windows gleam
with jewels and costly things that men buy for their
mistresses. Ten thousand public women parade – for
your true Bucarestian boasts that his city supports
more prostitutes in proportion than any other four
cities in the world combined....

To look at it all you would imagine that Bucarest
was as ancient as Sofia or Belgrade. The white stone
weathers so swiftly under the hot, dry sun, the oily

rich soil bears such a mellowing abundance of vegetation, life is so complex and sophisticated – yet thirty years ago there was nothing here but a wretched village, some old churches, and an older monastery which was the seat of a princely family. Bucarest is a get-rich city, and modern Rumanian civilization is like that – a mushroom growth of thirty years. The fat plain is one of the greatest grain-growing regions in the world, and there are mountains covered with fine timber; but the mainspring of wealth is the oil region. There are oil kings and timber kings and land kings, quickly and fabulously wealthy. It costs more to live in Bucarest than in New York.

There is nothing original about the city, nothing individual. Everything is borrowed. A dinky little German King lives in a dinky little palace that looks like a French Prefecture, surrounded by a pompous little court. The government is modelled on that of Belgium. Although all titles of nobility except in the King's immediate family were abolished years ago, many people call themselves "Prince" and "Count" because their forefathers were Moldavian and Wallachian boyars; not to speak of the families who trace their descent from the Emperors of Byzantium! Poets and artists and musicians and doctors and lawyers and politicians have all studied in Paris – and of late Vienna, Berlin, or Munich. Cubism is more cubic and futurism more futuristic in Rumania than at home. Frenchified little policemen bully the marketbound peasants, who dare to drive across the Calea Victoriei and interrupt the procession of kept women. Cabarets and music-halls are like the less amusing places on Montmartre; you can see Revues based on dull French ones, copies of risqué comedies straight from the Theatre Antoine, or the National Theatre – which imitates the Comédie Française, and looks like the Municipal Theatre at Lyons. A surface and without charm. coating of French frivolity covers everything – without meaning and without charm.

If you want to infuriate a Rumanian, you need only speak of his country as a Balkan state.

"Balkan!" he cries. "Balkan! Rumania is not a Balkan state. How dare you confuse us with half-savage Greeks or Slavs! We are Latins."

One is never allowed to forget that; the newspapers insist every day that Rumanians are Latins – every day there is a reference to "our brothers, the

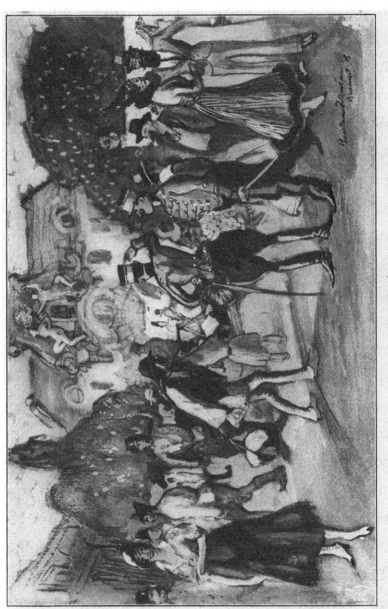

EVERY DAY THE CALEA VICTORIEI IN BUCAREST LOOKS LIKE THIS.

Illustration by Boardman Robinson
from *The War in Eastern Europe*

French, or the Spaniards, or the Italians" – but really of purer blood than these "brothers," for the Rumanians are descendants of Roman veterans colonized in Transylvania by the Emperor Trajan. Some local writers complacently insist that Rumania is the inheritor of the Roman Empire; in a square in Bucarest there is a fountain showing Romulus and Remus suckled by the wolf, and some of the public buildings are adorned with the Insignia, the Fasces, the Eagle, and "S.P.Q.R." But those Roman colonists may have been originally drafted into the legions from Tarsus, or the suburbs of Jerusalem, or south Germany. Add to that the blood of the native Dacians, a strong Slavic strain, Magyar, Vlaque, and a great deal of gypsy, and you have the Rumanian.... He speaks a Latin language strongly impregnated with Slavic and Asiatic roots – an inflexible tongue to use, and harsh and unmusical to the ear. And he has Latin traits: excitability, candor, wit, and a talent for hysterical argument in critical situations. He is lazy and proud, like a Spaniard, but without a Spaniard's flavor; skeptical and libertine, like a Frenchman, but without a Frenchman's taste; melodramatic and emotional, like an Italian, without Italian charm. One good observer

has called Rumanians "bad Frenchmen," and another "Italianized gypsies." Shopkeepers and cabmen
and waiters in restaurants are thieving and ungra-
cious; if they can't cheat you they fly into an ugly rage
and scream like angry monkeys. How many times
have Rumanian friends said to me: "Don't go to so-
and-so's shop; he is a Rumanian and will cheat you.
Find a German or French place."

It will be said that I have judged Rumanians by
the people of Bucarest, and that Bucarest is not all
Rumania. But I insist that the metropolis reflects the
dominant traits of any nation – that Paris is essentially French, Berlin essentially Prussian, and Bucarest thoroughly Rumanian. Sometimes there are
peasants on the street; the men in white linen trou-
sers, and shirts that fall to their knees, embroidered
in delicate designs of flowers, the women in richly
decorated linen skirts and blouses of drawn work ex-
quisitely worked in color, chains of gold coins hang-
ing around their necks. They fit into the comic-opera
scheme of things. But one hour by automobile from
Bucarest you come upon a village where the people
live in burrows in the ground, covered with roofs of
dirt and straw. The ground their burrows are dug in

Alexandru Marghiloman

is owned by a boyar – a landowning noble – who keeps a racing stable in France, and they till his land for him. Two per cent of the population can read and write. There is no school there. Several years ago the proprietor himself built a school for his people, on condition that the government would take it over and support it; for three years now it has been used as a storehouse.

These peasants eat nothing but corn – not because they are vegetarians, but because they are too poor to eat meat. And the church provides frequent fasts, which are the subject of laudatory comments on "frugality and thrift" by satisfied landowners. The peasants are very religious, or superstitious, whichever you want to call it. For instance, they believe that if a man dies without a lighted candle in his hand to guide him through the dark corridors of death, he will not reach heaven. Now many people do die suddenly without the lighted candle; and here is where the church comes in. The country priest charges the dead man's family eighty francs to get him into heaven without the candle, and a certain sum yearly to keep him there. The priest also takes advantage of the vampire legend – a superstition, widely believed in

Hungary, the Balkans, and south Russia. If a peasant dies and others from his family or village follow in quick succession, the priest suggests that the dead man's spirit is a vampire. To lay this murdering ghost, the body must be exhumed in the dead of night (for it is strictly forbidden by Rumanian criminal law) and the heart torn out by an ordained priest, who drives a wooden peg through it. For this he charges a hundred francs.

Once I went north on a night train which carried the Crown Prince's private car. It was a cold night, with a wind that ate into your bones. Yet all night long we looked from our window upon a line of wretched peasants standing beside the track, one every quarter of a mile, ragged and shivering, holding torches above their heads to do honor to their prince....

Never was a country so ripe for revolution. More than fifty per cent of the arable land is owned by less than ten per cent of the country's landowners – some four and a half thousand big proprietors out of a population of seven and a half millions, seven-eighths of whom are working peasants; and this in spite of the fact that the government has been breaking up the big estates and selling land to the people since 1864. The boyars and great landholders seldom live on their estates. Indeed, it is all they can do to keep up their hotels in Paris and Vienna, their houses in Bucarest, their villas at Nice, Constantza, and Sinaia, their winters on the Riviera, art galleries, racing stables, and general blowing of money in the four quarters of the world. One family I met posed as great humanitarians because they provided mud huts for their people, and paid them twenty cents a day – with the cost of living almost what it is in New Jersey. Add to this hopeless condition of affairs the fact that all voters in Rumania are divided into three classes, on the basis of their incomes, so that about one hundred peasants' votes equal one rich man's vote. There have been several revolutions in Rumania, the last one purely agrarian, in 1907; but since the conscript army system exists, it is easy to order peasants in the south to shoot down their northern brothers, and vice versa. You have only to see the Rumanian peasants, gentle, submissive, with almost effeminate dress, manners – even their national songs and dances are pretty and soft – to realize how frightful the pressure that would force them to revolt.

What is the trend of Rumanian public opinion? There is no public opinion in Rumania. The peasants will fight for whatever their masters decide will give them the greatest country to exploit. It is simply another demonstration of how military service delivers a nation bound hand and foot to ambitious politicians. So one must ask the politicians, and they will reply that Rumania will join the side that satisfies "national aspirations" – as they call cupidity in the Balkans.

Now the Rumanians came originally from Transylvania, and settled the flat plain north of the Danube which includes Bessarabia, and stretches eastward to the Black Sea. A race of herders and farmers, they spread far; southern Bucovina is full of Rumanians, and they are found in compact groups throughout Bulgaria, Serbia, the Banat, Macedonia, and Greece. The most civilized section, Transylvania, was early drawn into the Hungarian kingdom; Bucovina was a present from the Turkish Sultan to the Emperor Joseph, and Bessarabia, twice Rumanian, was finally taken by Russia as the price of Rumanian independence after the battle of Plevna. And although many people now alive remember the passing of the

King Carol I of Romania

Russian armies that freed Rumania from the Turk, they cannot forget the two million Rumanians who fell under the Russian yoke. It was partially to make up for the loss of that great province that Rumania stabbed Bulgaria in the back in 1913, and took away Silistra, where there was no Rumanian population. When there is no other reason for territorial conquest, this kind of "national aspirations" is excused by Balkanians on "strategical grounds."

Bessarabia was forcibly Russianized. The upper classes, of course, easily became Russian, but the prohibition of the Rumanian language in schools and churches had the effect of driving the peasants out of both – of making a brutalized and degraded race, who have lost all connection with or knowledge of their mother country.

In Transylvania, the birthplace of the race, and the Banat beyond, there are some three million Rumanians. But there, in spite of the desperate Hungarian campaign to Magyarize the people as the Russians did in Bessarabia, the racial feeling is strong and growing. The Transylvanians are rich and civilized; when the Rumanian tongue was banned in the higher schools and the churches, they fought a stubborn fight, crossing the mountains into Rumania for education, and spreading the nationalist propaganda at home and abroad so thoroughly that every Rumanian knows and feels for his oppressed brothers on the other side of the Carpathians, and you can travel across Hungary as far as Buda-Pesth and beyond without speaking any language but Rumanian.

So the "national aspirations" of Rumania, on "ethnographical grounds," include Bessarabia, Bucovina, Transylvania, and the Banat; and I have also seen a map in Bucarest, colored to show that Macedonia should really belong to Rumania, because the majority of the population are Rumanians!

All this does not excite the peasant to the verge of war on any side. But there is a mortal wrestling match going on between pro-Teuton and pro-Ally politicians. How many obscure lawyers are now getting rich in the limelight of political prominence! In the Balkans politics is largely a personal matter; newspapers are the organs of individual men who have jockeyed themselves to be party leaders, in countries where a new party is born every hour over a glass of beer in the nearest café. For instance, *La Politique* is

the organ of the millionaire Marghiloman, lately chief
of the Conservative party and only partially deposed.
He was once so pro-French that it is said he used to
send his laundry to Paris – but the Germans got him.
His pro-Ally constituents split off under Mr. Filipescu, violently anti-German, whose organ is the
Journal des Balkans.... Then there is the *Independence Roumaine*, property of the family of Mr. Bratianu, the premier – who was pro-German at the beginning of the war, but has become mildly pro-Ally –
chief of the Liberal party now in power. And *La Rou-
manie*, mouthpiece of Mr. Take Ionescu, the leader of
the Conservative Democrats, who is the most powerful force in the country on the side of the Entente
Powers. The Conservatives are the great proprietors;
the Liberals are the capitalists; the Conservative
Democrats are about the same as our Progressives,
and the peasants' Socialist Agrarian party doesn't
count. But all internal programmes were forgotten at
the question: On which side shall Rumania enter the
war?

Two years ago old King Carol summoned a coun-
cil of ministers and party leaders at Sinaia, and made
a speech advocating immediate entrance on the side

Take Ionescu

of the Central Powers. But when a vote was taken, only one man present was with the King. It was the first time his royal will had ever been thwarted, and a few days later he died without returning to the capital. Ferdinand, the present King, is in the same predicament, and, what is more, he has an English queen.... It is a great game being fought over the heads of the King and the people by powerful financial interests, and the ambitions of political jugglers.

Meanwhile, a steady stream of Russian gold has poured into willing pockets, and the methodical Teutons have been creating public sentiment in their own inimitable way. Thousands of Germans and Austrians descended upon Bucarest in holiday attire, their wallets bulging with money. The hotels were full of them. They took the best seats at every play, violently applauding things German and Rumanian, hissing things French and English. They printed pro-German newspapers and distributed them free to the peasants. Restaurants and gambling casinos, dear to the Rumanian heart, were bought by them. German goods at reduced prices flooded the shops. They supported all the girls, bought all the champagne, corrupted all the government functionaries they could reach.... A nation-wide agitation was started about "our poor oppressed brothers in Russian Bessarabia"– in order to divert attention from Transylvania and stir up anti-Russian feeling.

To the Rumanian Government, Germany and Austria offered Bessarabia, including even Odessa, and Bucovina would also be ceded if she insisted. The Allies offered Transylvania, the Banat, and the Bucovina plateau north of her frontier. Although there was much talk in the press about "redeeming lost Bessarabia," the Bessarabian question was really not a vital one, while the Transylvanian question was burning and immediate. Moreover, the Rumanians know that Russia is a coming nation, and that forty years from now, even if defeated in this war, she will be there just the same, and stronger; while Austria-Hungary is an old and disintegrating empire, whose drive will be no longer eastward.

Three times since the war began Rumania tentatively agreed with the Allies to enter – and three times she drew back: once in the early spring, when Russia

Ion I.C. Bratianu

was on the Carpathians, and again when Italy entered. The last time was when I saw Mr. Take Ionescu at midnight of the day that Bulgaria signed her agreement with Turkey.

"I think Bulgaria has chosen her side," he said very gravely. "We are not such babies as to believe that Turkey would give up any territory for nothing. The Central Powers will drive through Serbia – only we can stop that. And I am in a position to tell you that Serbia can claim our help if she is attacked. The Austrians have closed their frontier to us, and four hundred thousand men are said to be massed ready to march on Bucarest. It is a bluff – a bluff to force the resignation of the Bratianu cabinet, and the calling of Mr. Marghiloman to form a ministry – which would mean a German policy. Even if the Bratianu cabinet fell – which I doubt, for he is not for war – only he and the King working together could pave the way for Marghiloman. And that is impossible."

Three weeks later the German drive on Serbia began; but once more Rumania held aloof.

THE RIGHTS OF
SMALL NATIONS*

I was having my passport viséd in the Bulgarian consulate at Bucarest, when Frank came in on the same errand. I knew at once that he was an American. The tides of immigration had washed his blood, the Leyendecker brothers had influenced the cut of his nose and jaw, and his look and walk were direct and unsophisticated. He was blond, youthful, "clean-cut." Beneath the tweed imitation English clothes that Rumanian tailors affect, his body was the body of a college sprinter not yet gone soft, as economically built as a wild animal's.

As instinctively, too, as an animal, for he was not observant, he flair'd in me a kinsman, and said "Hello" with the superior inflection of one Anglo-Saxon greeting another in the presence of foreign and

---

*from John Reed, *Daughter of the Revolution and Other Stories*, edited by Floyd Dell, (New York, 1927), pp. 75-80.

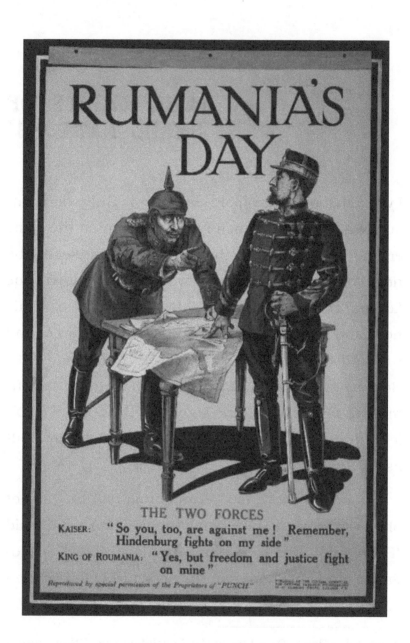

inferior peoples. He was a communicative boy, too long away from home to be suspicious of Americans. If I were going by the one-thirty train to Sofia, he said, we might travel together. He himself had been working for the Romano-Americano Oil Company – a subsidiary alias for Standard Oil – for two years, in the Rumanian petroleum fields near Ploeshti. And as we walked down the street together he said that he was going to England to enlist in the army and fight.

"What for?" I cried out in astonishment.

"Well," he said earnestly, looking at me with troubled eyes and shaking his head, "there's a bunch of Englishmen out at Ploeshti, and they told me all about it. I don't care – perhaps it's foolish, like everybody says out in our camp – but I can't help it. I've got to go. I think it was a dirty trick to violate the neutrality of Belgium."

"The neutrality of Belgium!" said I, with a sense of awe at the preposterous possibilities of human nature.

"Yes," he rushed on, "it makes me hot to think of a little country like Belgium and a big bully of a country like Germany. It's a damn shame! England is fighting for the rights of small nations, and I don't see how anybody can keep out of it that's got any guts!"

Some hours later I saw him on the station platform, talking to a thin, plain girl in a yellow cotton dress, who wept and powdered her nose simultaneously. His face was flushed and frowning, and he spat out his words the way a strong man does when he's angry at his dog, his servant, or his wife. The girl wept monotonously; sometimes she touched him with a timid, hungry gesture, but he shook off her hand.

He caught sight of me and brusquely quitted her, coming over with a shamefaced expression. He was evidently worried and exasperated. "Be with you as soon as I get rid of this damn woman!" he said, brutally masculine. "They can't leave a man alone, can they?"

Lighting a cigarette, he swaggered back to where she stood staring fixedly out along the track, her handkerchief crammed in her mouth, making a desperate effort to control herself. She had on excessively high-heeled slippers, such as Rumanian street-walkers wore that year, and carried a leather wrist-bag; everything about her was shabby. Her young breasts were flat, starved, and her knotted hair thin and dull. I knew that only a very unattractive girl could fail to make a living in Bucarest, where they boast more

King Ferdinand of Romania

prostitutes to the square male than any other city in
the world.

Her eyes involuntarily leaped to his face; she began to shake. Frank dug into his pockets in a surly
way, pulled out a roll of banknotes, and peeled off
two. The girl stiffened, went white and rigid; her eyes
blazed. His outstretched hand with the money was
like a loaded gun. But suddenly the dull red crept up
her cheek like pain, and she clutched the bills and
burst into violent sobbing. After all, she had to live.

My compatriot threw me a comic, despairing look
and glowered at her. "What do you want?" he growled
in harsh, unpleasant Rumanian. "I don't owe you anything. What are you bawling for? Run along home
now. Good-by." He gave her a little clumsy push. She
took two or three steps and stopped, as if she had no
power to move further. And some instinct or some
memory gave him a flash of understanding. He put
his hands on her shoulders suddenly, and kissed her
on the mouth. "Good-by," said the girl brokenly, and
she ran.

We rattled south over the flat, hot plain, past
wretched villages of mud huts roofed with filthy
straw, halting long at little stations where the docile
gaunt peasants in ragged white linen gaped stupidly

at the train. The rich hectic whiteness of Bucarest vanished abruptly out of a world where people starved in hopeless misery.

"I don't understand women," Frank was saying. "You can't get rid of 'em when you're finished. Now I had that girl for about nine months. I gave her a good home to live in and better food to eat than she ever got in her life, and money – why, she spent on dresses and hats and postage stamps about a hundred and fifty dollars. But do you think she had any gratitude? Not her. When I got sick of her she thought she had a mortgage on the place – said she wasn't going to go. I had to push her out. Then afterward she began to write me hard-luck letters – nothing but a game to get money out of me. Fall for it? Of course I didn't fall for it. I'm not so easy as that! This morning I ran into her when I came up to take the train, and I swear I couldn't shake that skirt all day. Crying-ugh!"

"Where did you get her?" I asked.

"Her? Oh, I just picked her up on the street in Ploeshti.... You bet she'd never been with another fellow! That's dangerous."

He looked at me, and a vague uncomfortableness made him desirous of justifying himself. "You see, out in the oil-fields every fellow has his own house. And you've got to eat and get washing done and have a clean place to live, of course. So everybody gets a girl to cook, wash, take care of the house and live with him. It's hard to get one who suits you all around. I've tried three, and I know fellows who've had six or eight; take 'em in try 'em, kick 'em out.

"Pay? Why, you don't pay 'em anything. First place they live with you; don't they? And then they've got a house and food, and you buy their clothes for them. Nothing doing in the salary line. They might beat it with the money. No, that's the way you keep 'em on their good behavior. If they don't do what they're told, you shut down on their clothes.".

I wanted to know if any of these ménages lasted.

"Well," said Frank, "there's Jordan. He's got the most beautiful house in our camp: you ought to see that place. But of course he leads a pretty lonely life, because only the unmarried boys ever come to see him; sometimes a married man, but never with his wife. Jordan's been living with a girl for eleven years – a Rumanian girl he took just like we take ours – and of course nobody will have anything to do with him. He's the cleverest guy in the company, that man, but they can't promote him while he lives like that. A high official out here has got to be more or less of a social light, you know. So he's sat there for years and seen man after man that isn't worth a quarter what he is, passed over his head."

"Why doesn't he marry her?"

"What!" said Frank, surprised. "That kind of a woman? After her living with him all that time? Nobody would associate with her. She's not decent.

"Doesn't it hurt your prospects to live with women?"

"Oh, us! No, that's different. Everybody thinks it's all right, so long as we don't go around with the girls in public. You see, we're young fellows. It's only when you get about thirty that you must get married. I'm twenty-five."

"Then in five years –"

He nodded his yellow head. "I'll begin to think about getting a wife. But that's purely a business proposition. There's no use marrying – of course a real man has to have a woman once in a while, I know that, but I mean there's no use tying yourself up – unless you can get something good out of it. I'm going to pick a good-looker, with no scandal about her and a social pull that will help me in my job. Down South there's plenty of girls like that. I don't need her money

– I can make a pretty good salary in a couple of years; and, besides, if your wife has an income of her own she's liable to want to do what she pleases. Don't you think so?"

"I think that's a rotten way to look at it," said I with heat. "If I lived with a girl, whether we were married or not, I'd make her my equal, financially and every other way." Frank laughed. "And as for your plans for marriage, how can you marry any one you don't love?"

"Oh, love!" Frank shrugged his shoulders with annoyance and looked out of the window. "Hell, if you're going to get sentimental...."

1915

ROUMANIAN SOLDIER FINDS HIS WAY FROM RUSSIAN FRONT TO AMERICA*

Incident of How East Side, Haven of Many Nationalities, Proves It Really Is Nearest Point in U.S. to European Conflict.

The east side is nearer to Europe than the rest of New York. The poets, dramatists, musicians, follow the European tradition, and are great men in their own tongues, among their own peoples.

Events of the foreign world reverberate loudest on the east side, and find their truest interpretation in Yiddish, or Italian, or Polish, or Roumanian. And during all these three years the great war has been very close to the east side, where almost every family has had a son, brother or husband in the trenches.

Sometimes these breathless summer nights I play Haroun-al-Raschid. I take off my collar, roll up my

---

*from *New York Mail*, 24 July 1917, pp. 1, 4.

sleeves and wander down East Houston street. A wave of heat, radiated by those iron streets and from that welter of sweating humanity; the immense, restless roar of hot people, punctuated by shrieks of children and the wailing of babies; the nasal shouts of soft drink and ice cream peddlers; the myriad brilliant little shop fronts; the long pushcarts, their yellow flares ringed with alien faces – all these things engulf me like a sea.

Last night, quite by chance, I found myself in Eldridge street, where many Roumanians live. Now Eldridge street was as steamy-hot as a Turkish bath. It was littered with papers and refuse, and it stunk. An incredible number of children boiled noisily in the middle of the street, or rolled in whatever gutter puddles the last thunder shower had left.

SOME TRYING TO SLEEP

All, the fire escapes blossomed with bedclothes, where already – for it was late – figures writhed and tried in vain to sleep. Out of every window hung half-clad shoulders. In every doorway the girls and boys sat closely wedged, screaming and giggling. And the drooping elders slumped upon chairs placed in the gutter, their feet upon the curb.

From the steps of one building came a rapid stream of Roumanian – the language which sounds like nothing so much as a slack violin string. Then a harsh, female voice, in the accents of Times square, translating:

"He says the officers – the cap'n and both lootenants, he says – when the Austri'n troops commenced to charge acrost the valley, they both beat it. He says the general was a willy-boy, an' painted his face ——"

On the top step sat a very old man, whose enormous white head seemed too heavy for his bird-like neck. Next below was a ruddy fellow of middle age, in rough working clothes, his shirt open at the throat. He it was who was talking. Around him were grouped two men and three women of about his own age, and it was one of the women who was translating.

Three girls and two boys, ranging in age from about ten to sixteen, squeezed "Iassy," he replied quickly, and grinned.

"But that's in Roumania!" I objected.

The girl broke in impatiently. "You wasn't here when he told about that," she said. "You see he got tired of the war and so he thought he'd come over here and git out of it."

RODE THE RODS.

"Deserted?" I asked.

"Naw, just quit," she grinned, "Well, he started back into Rooshia walking. I was only a kid when I left the old country, so I don't remember much about the place. Well, then a train come along and he rode the rods to a town called Kishineff, where he got some rube to sell him a suit of clothes. Sure. And in this town was where he heard about the Rooshian revolution."

Aw, say, Bertha," whined the boy, "we bin all over that. Ain't you ever goin' to get done."

Bertha turned on him. "That's a fine way to act, she said, "when your uncle's jest come from the war the first night. This gemman didn't hear that part." She went on:

"Well, a feller in the town told him a couple of words which meant 'free Rooshia,' and that was all the Rooshian he had. So he went along up north, and every time he wanted anything he just said free Rooshia, and they give it to him. When he was hungry he went up to a restaurant or a house and pounded

CROSSING THE PRUTH IN A FLAT-BOTTOMED SCOW, HALF FULL OF WATER.

Illustration by Boardman Robinson
from *The War in Eastern Europe*

his chest and says, 'free Rooshia;' same when he wanted a ride – and also when they asked him for his papers."

"Papers, he says, giving himself a knock, wot d'ye mean, papers? Ain't this free Rooshia?"

"And so at last he come to Petrograd, and from there he got a job on a little boat which took some people down to Copenhagen. And then he was a sto'way on a Danish boat which come in here this morning and he found us by the priest at the Roumanian church."

Now the soldier was talking again. He was telling how the Roumanian army set fire to the Ploeshti oil fields, and the tall, smoky columns of flame that stood up roaring over the countryside as the soldiers marched away.

"South of Ploeshti?" interrupted the old man, in a squeaky voice, jerking himself erect. "South? By the little hill."

"Yes, yes father," Bertha answered. "He says it was where the little farm was."

HAD OWNED THE FARM

The old man said something in Roumanian and then sighed and changed into English. "Ai," he said, "ai, ai. It was a pretty leetle farm. Gif to me by Boyar Filipescu. Not many peasants in de old country with farms belong to dem. I remember——"

"Yes, yes, father," cried Bertha, impatiently. "I know. You remember before they struck oil. They bought your little farm for nothing – and it worth a fortune."

But the soldier was speaking again, telling them that all of that was gone now – that there was no more Roumania.

"But there will be again some day," he continued brightly. There was no response from the rest of the family except from the old man, who moved his head backward and forward with a tremulous smile. As for the children, it was plainly a matter of indifference to them whether there should ever be a Roumania or not. They had Americanitis, and they had it strong.

Pretty soon everybody rose, and Bertha addressed me. "We're all going down to the rathskeller across the street and drink a little Roumanian wine," said she. "Want to come along?" As we went I saw the children stealthily scattering.

It was a filthy, smelly little cellar, with long lace curtains at the subterranean windows and immaculate sawdust on the floor. We all took our places at a long table, and they put before us bottles of raw sweet Roumanian wine and siphons.

PLAY STRANGE MUSIC

Then the orchestra struck up – a gypsy open piano, like an xylophone, and a violin. Two dirty, swarthy fellows played, beginning with a very commonplace waltz played in a very ordinary manner. And then, half way through the piece, they suddenly swung gently off into that old gypsy jig music – suggestive, sensual, twitching at the feet, wild, abandoned – the strange music that is like a drug: which is heard all over the Hungarian plain and eastward, even up into Russia.

The conversation dropped unnoticed. The young soldier's mouth parted in a smile, his eyes closed. He swayed. The musicians played, swaying faster and faster, wilder and wilder, their eyes closed. The old man suddenly began to move his shoulders as one moves machinery long rusted, and all at once he gave a yell, and then laughed with pure delight.

And then abruptly the soldier had bounded to his feet, kicked the chairs out of the way and begun a Roumanian peasant dance, lifting his hand over his head.

And suddenly Bertha, the unmarried one, threw her head down upon her folded arms on the table and began to sob.

"Oh," she cried, passionately, "I hate this place."

On the lower step the old grandmother sat in a rocking chair out in the gutter, her uneasy, sleeping head rolled sideways on her breast.

I climbed through the children and sat beside the old man on the top step. And they made way for me casually, nor hardly even glanced up. So terribly crowded is it on Eldridge street that of necessity all men are neighbors.

TALKS OF BATTLE

The young man talked on, gesturing, and his sister translated. Now he was telling of battle – and telling it in the words of one who has seen battle. The oldest boy and girl were restless. They kept shifting about on their seats and peering up and down the street. The girl made covert signs to a boy on the opposite sidewalk.

It was a dramatic group. The old man and woman, peasants who had pulled up their roots from the rich fields of Roumania and emigrated to America twelve years before. Their lives would always be in the past; their eyes turned backward. Then the two daughters and one son – the son and one daughter with wife and husband, and one daughter, the translator, unmarried. This second generation had been born abroad and were still half-Roumanian, speaking both languages.

And finally the children, entirely American, speaking no Roumanian, contemptuous of "foreigners" and "foreign" things; dressed with smart cheapness, following the movies, humming and whistling the blatant "jazz" tunes of Broadway. (All this I elicited little by little.)

"He has been in the war?" I asked, pointing to the stranger.

"Sure has he," responded the big woman. "He jest hit here this morning." She addressed him shrilly.

"Stockholm," said the man, turning and looking at me, "Stockholm."

I was astonished. "You mean he came by Stockholm?" I asked. "But where did he come from?"

The man guessed at my question.

LAST DAYS WITH
JOHN REED

A LETTER FROM
LOUISE BRYANT

Louise Bryant

LAST DAYS WITH JOHN REED

A Letter from Louise Bryant*

Moscow, November 14, 1920

Dear Max: – I knew you would want details and a story for the *Liberator* – but I did not have either the strength or the courage. As it is – I will be able to write only a very incoherent letter and you may take from it what you wish. Jack's death and my strenuous underground trip to Russia and the weeks of horror in the typhus hospital have quite broken me. At the funeral, I suffered a very severe heart attack which by the merest scratch I survived. Specialists have agreed that I have strained my heart because of the long days and nights I watched beside Jack's bed and that it is enlarged and may not get ever well again. They

---

*Letter to Max Eastman, published in *The Liberator*, 21 January 1921, pp. 11-14.

do not agree, however, on the time it will take for another attack. I write you all these stupid things because I have to face them myself and because it must be part of the letter. The American and German doctors give me a year or even two, the Russians only months. I have to take stimulants and I am in not a bit of pain. I think I have better recuperative powers than they believe – but, anyway, it is a small matter. I once promised Jack that I would put all his works in order in case of his death. I will come home if I get stronger and do so.

All that I write now seems part of a dream. I am in no pain at all and I find it impossible to believe that Jack is dead or that he will not come into this very room any moment.

Jack was ill twenty days. Only two nights, when he was calmer, did I even lie down. Spotted typhus is beyond description, the patient wastes to nothing under your eyes.

But I must go back to tell you how I found Jack after my illegal journey across the world. I had to skirt Finland, sail twelve days in the Arctic ocean, hide in a fisherman's shack four days to avoid the police with a Finnish officer and a German, both under sentence of death in their own countries. When I did reach Soviet territory, I was at the opposite end of Russia from Jack. When I reached Moscow he was in Baku at the Oriental Congress. Civil war raged in the Ukraine. A military wire reached him and he came back in an armored train. On the morning of September 15th, he ran shouting into my room. A month later he was dead.

We had only one week together before he went to bed, and we were terribly happy to find each other. I found him older and sadder and grown strangely gentle and aesthetic. His clothes were just rags. He was so impressed with the suffering around him that he would take nothing for himself. I felt shocked and almost unable to reach the pinnacle of fervor he had attained.

The effects of the terrible experience in the Finnish gaol were all too apparent. He told me of his cell, dark and cold and wet. Almost three months of solitary confinement and only raw fish to eat. Sometimes he was delirious and imagined me dead. Sometimes he expected to die himself, so he wrote on books and everywhere a little verse:

Thinking and dreaming
Day and night and day
Yet cannot think one bitter thought away –
That we have lost each other
You and I...

But walking in the park, under the white birch trees and talking through brief, happy nights, death and separation seemed very far away.

We visited together Lenin, Trotsky, Kaminev, Enver Pasha, Bela Kun, we saw the Ballet and Prince Igor and the new and old galleries.

He was consumed with a desire to go home. I felt how tired and ill he was – how near a breakdown and tried to persuade him to rest. The Russians told me that he often worked twenty hours a day. Early in his sickness I asked him to promise me that he would rest before going home since it only meant going to prison. I felt prison would be too much for him. I remember he looked at me in a strange way and said, "My dear little Honey, I would do anything I could for you, but don't ask me to be a coward." I had not meant it so. I felt so hurt that I burst into tears and said he could go and I would go with him anywhere by the next train, to any death or any suffering. He smiled so happily then. And all the days that followed he held me tightly by the hand. I could not leave him because he would shout for me. I have a feeling now that I have no right to be alive.

Of the illness I can scarcely write – there was so much pain. I only want you all to know how he fought for his life. He would have died days before but for the fight he made. The old peasant nurses used to slip out to the Chapel and pray for him and burn a candle for his life. Even they were touched and they see men die in agony every hour.

He was never delirious in the hideous way most typhus patients are. He always knew me and his mind was full of poems and stories and beautiful thoughts. He would say, "You know how it is when you go to Venice. You ask people – Is this Venice? – just for the pleasure of hearing the reply." He would tell me that the water he drank was full of little songs. And he related, like a child, wonderful experiences we had together and in which we were very brave.

Five days before he died his right side was paralyzed. After that he could not speak. And so we watched through days and nights and days hoping against all hope. Even when he died I did not believe it. I must have been there hours afterwards still talking to him and holding his hands.

Portrait of John Reed by Robert Hallowell

And then there came a time when his body lay in state with all military honor, in the Labor Temple, guarded by fourteen soldiers from the Red Army. Many times I went there and saw the soldiers standing stiffly, their bayonets gleaming under the lights and the red star of Communism on their military caps.

Jack lay in a long silver coffin banked with flowers and streaming banners. Once the soldiers uncovered it for me so I might touch the high white forehead with my lips for the last time.

On the day of the funeral we gathered in the great hall where he lay. I have very few impressions of that day. It was cold and the sky dark, snow fell as we began to march. I was conscious of how people cried and of how the banners floated and how the wailing heart-breaking Revolutionary funeral hymn, played by a military band, went on forever and ever.

The Russians let me take my grief in my own way, since they felt I had thrown all caution to the winds in going to the hospital. On that day I felt very proud and even strong. I wished to walk according to the Russian custom, quite by myself after the hearse. And in the Red Square I tried to stand facing the speakers with a brave face. But I was not brave at all and fell on the ground and could not speak or cry.

I do not remember the speeches. I remember more the broken notes of the speakers' voices. I was aware that after a long time they ceased and the banners began to dip back and forth in salute. I heard the first shovel of earth go rolling down and then something snapped in my brain. After an eternity I woke up in my own bed. Emma Goldman was standing there and Berkman, and two doctors and a tall young officer from the Red Army. They were whispering and so I went to sleep again.

But I have been in the Red Square since then – since that day all those people came to bury in all honor our dear Jack Reed. I have been there in the busy afternoon when all Russia hurries by, horses and sleighs and bells and peasants carrying bundles, soldiers singing on their way to the front. Once some of the soldiers came over to the grave. They took off their hats and spoke very reverently. "What a good fellow he was!" said one. "He came all the way across the world for us." "He was one of ours——" In another moment they shouldered their guns and went on again.

I have been there under the stars with a great longing to lie down beside the frozen flowers and the metallic wreaths and not wake up. How easy it would be!

I send greetings to all old friends.

Good luck to all of you.

Louise

Suggested Reading

Gelb, Barbara. *So Short a Time: A Biography of John Reed and Louise Bryant.* New York: W.W. Norton & Co., Inc., 1973.

Hicks, Granville. *John Reed: The Making of a Revolutionary.* New York: The MacMillan Company, 1936.

Hovey, Tamara. *John Reed: Witness to Revolution.* Los Angeles: George Sand Books, 1975.

Reed, John. *An Anthology.* Moscow: Progress Publishers, 1966.

Reed, John. *Insurgent Mexico.* New York: International Publishers, 1969.

Reed, John. *10 Days that Shook the World.* New York: International Publishers, 1967.

Reed, John. *10 zile care au zguduit lumea.* Bucharest, 1957.

Reed, John. *Why Political Democracy Must Go.* Ed. A.K. Brackob. Las Vegas: Gaudium Publishing, 2021.

Rosenstone, Robert A. *Romantic Revolutionary: A Biography of John Reed.* New York: Alfred A Knopf, 1975.

Shannon, David A. *The Socialist Party of America: A History.* New York: The MacMillan Company, 1955.

Stuart, John, ed. *The Education of John Reed.* New York: International Publishers, 1955.

Tuck, Jim. *Pancho Villa and John Reed: Two Faces of Romantic Revolution.* Tucson: University of Arizona Press, 1984.

Wolfe, Bertram D. *Strange Communists I Have Known.* New York: Bantam Books, 1967.

CENTER FOR
Romanian
S T U D I E S

The mission of the Center for Romanian Studies is to
promote knowledge of the history, literature, and culture
of Romania to an international audience.
For more information contact us at
info@centerforromanianstudies.com

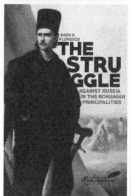

Check out these and other great titles at
CenterforRomanianStudies.com